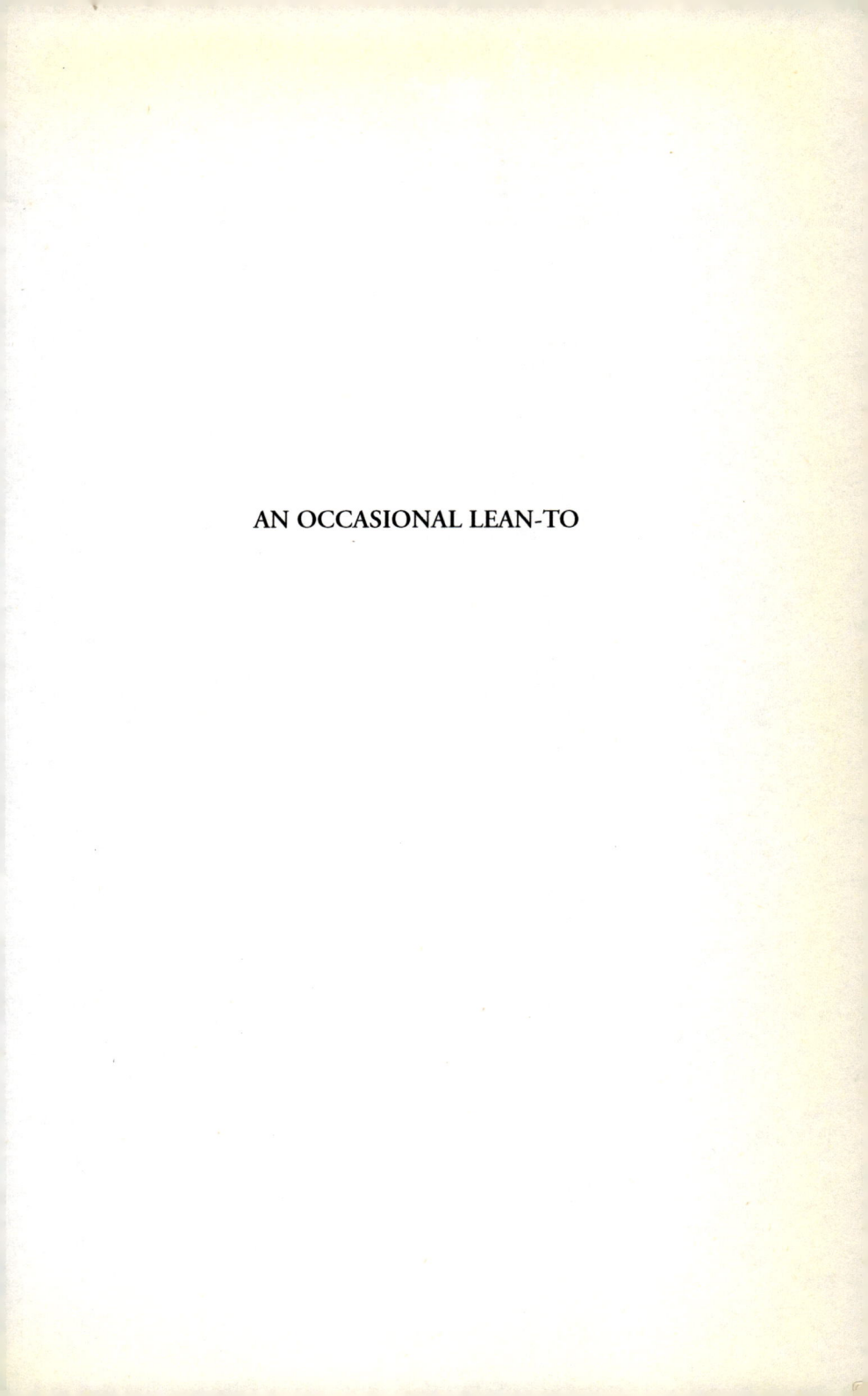

AN OCCASIONAL LEAN-TO

AN OCCASIONAL LEAN-TO

IAN POPLE

2004

Published by Arc Publications
Nanholme Mill, Shaw Wood Road
Todmorden OL14 6DA, UK

© Ian Pople 2004

Design by Tony Ward
Print by Antony Rowe Ltd.,
Eastbourne, East Sussex

ISBN 1 900072 98 X

Cover illustration by Wendy Raphael

Thanks are due to
ACE North West
for an Individual Writer's Grant, 2000-1,
to the Warden and staff of St Deiniol's Library, Hawarden,
and to those who read this text in different versions,
in particular, Livi Michael and Edmund Prestwich.

The Publishers acknowledge financial
assistance from ACE Yorkshire

Editor for UK / Ireland: Jo Shapcott

Contents

Texts   7

An Occasional Lean-to
- 1 A genesis   19
- 2 '...them that are without'   27
- 3 '...in the seventh month...'   36
- 4 Midrash   46
- 5 '...one equal light...'   49
- 6 Penitential Psalms   59
- 7 'Somewhere or other inside his head there must be an angel'   68

Notes   77

Biographical note   79

Texts

i.m. Bishop John Vernon Taylor [1]

I

Below the plane, the sea
is smeared with pools; snow-
fields retreat from their

client lakes. Tomorrow,
only the hotel maid
will know on which

side the bed has been slept.
Outside, the sewage farm
will spool and spool.

Inside the hill-top
museum, a stone panther's
breaking a stone bear.

The busts of the goddess show
a circlet of hair and the same
face. Her marble hunting

dog is all muzzle and tension.
Her lions scratch and scratch
until the flesh unfolds.

The island has no cars,
but thirty eight entrees
and wasps that settle honied

cakes. Bougainvillea
drops its flowers to tumble
and dry upon the cobbles;

A wood wasp's died
among the ants. The woman
feeding chickens by

the dry stream bed,
keeps them caged
and will not give them names.

II

A village by the old sea
in older heat; open floors
and pillars of half-built houses

where boy-gangs go and cause
real damage. With catapults
and red bandannas, they'll

cicatrize a cheek, take out
a blameless eye. Small boys,
too, swim in the kelp that rocks

and washes by the jagged shore.
A toy can die, can be reborn,
can kill again. These things

that neither sex, nor family,
nor the company of dogs, nor
settling a Madonna deep in

sunlit sea can cure, to gather
on the shore, walk in, where socks
and shoes will stir the sand

until, beneath a knot of kicking
legs, water cloud and dazzle,
spillage of minerals, sheddings

of plant and beast, are those
who've come to map and navigate
towards the unhoused air.

III

The cyst of surprise; to be
in work late Saturday
afternoon. Deserted

massiveness of building.
On the late bus to the station,
as heat loosens from the city.

From the footbridge, a hare
on tracks that sort
and un-sort themselves.

Breeze-block exterior
with gulls and a blurred
clock tower. A train

in sunset, its grain
contains a man whistling,
doing up his tie, a woman

creaming her hands,
another in uncontrollable
sleep. The grain of the night-

train contains home
and sleep, showering off
the sweat, the walk from the station.

Over headlamps and street-
lamps, among the dark trees,
owls screech, once and again.

IV

Light that spreads evenly
on nictitating eyes,
gathers to a white chip.

Its pale iris
holds the breathing house.
The vivid nostrils

might seem spread
for an ants' nest or a wasp
among the cluttered branches.

Here, feeding boxes
matt-grey chipped
to black, and a perch wedged

in the far cage corner,
give the world a shape.
Perhaps the wire struts

provide a significant
other. Soon it'll
drill the house with its

screams, bobbing to wring
the cage, driving the humans
away from themselves.

V

Silent rooms where
a child is heard shouting
from a nearby street.

Just beyond, a squirrel
and a pigeon on the same branch
where leaves fill up

the rood screen of the tree.
Blue tits feed
on the broom's late flowers.

Among the long field-
corner grass, is a cat.
Out with the dog, you could

be anything and worldly
-wise. A pond floats
beside a rising wall.

VI

The man in the atelier sells
from under a fedora.
His smoke-filled voice

and long limbs gesture
that his painters are all
exiles. They specialize

in light, the sense of touch.
Sawdust pours
from the workbench, in the noise

and smell of the warming blade
and light through an ill-fitting
door that's jammed back

on harbour sunlight.
There's comfort in the sweat
of overalls, though the cuticle

on the right-hand thumb
is ripped and weeping. A sense
of places, wood fitting

wood, then nestling
canvas and the calm easel;
name, month, year.

VII

It wasn't the dew
across the grass, or that
glistening light, it was

simply the month of July
and a blue van beside
the shed. Above the quay

with its Friday lunchtime
smell and alleyway
spillage, beyond the field

gate where the ruck
-sack caught in thorns;
beyond the field drains

and cows working the pasture,
was the miscellany of olive
trees, pines and sky –

o ouranos,[2] and Mars moving
further west, the moon
shaved in the dance of clouds.

An Occasional Lean-to

*But the natural man receiveth not
the things of the Spirit of God:
for they are foolishness unto him.*
                    1 Corinthians 2:14

*The relation between us and God,
between this world and His world,
presses for recognition, but
the line of intersection is not self-evident.*
                    Karl Barth [3]

*To Ruth Sharman and
Michael Symmons Roberts*

1 A genesis

What moves before surf
in the tide are filaments
and lucid flesh, a swollen
green; particle and wave
hidden in debris that longs

to be ice. Water is a litter
worn from itself, from
continents in absentia,
subsistence farming
of matter. As we take

steps to hold what fluid
means in us, so the parachute
canopy becomes the plane
and the car, a lean-to
under splintering sky.

*

Small boy in a red hat
saw chaffinches, fungi,
a tree-creeper, butter bur,
and learnt to prise them
from his wildlife book.

We bent to bitter florets
of marsh marigold.
Anglers, hand over hand,
gathered skittering fish that
warped away from themselves

unable to recede to a light
they had only just been,
between carpet mill
and empty football ground,
in this pivot of water.

*

Driving past on the top
road, the wipers slow;
the self is uncertain,
untranscended,
an iron taste in the mouth.

Birds in white-grey
sky are filaments
of a darker world. Crows
at the unsettling twig,
rooks in vortices

of cantilevered flight,
are, perhaps, versions
of the go-between god;
the certain pigeon, a swallow
flying from the early plough.

*

This valley is distinct
and warm, made from ash,
conifers, laburnum,
crazed with paths
which sheep have cut.

The heron is open above
and apple blossom below;
though somewhere near
an engine seems to be
drowning. And this

is the testament; how
that sub-frame became
stranded beyond the field
gate and the plum tree
espaliered into life.

*

The gecko is important,
that runs the ceiling
for mosquitoes.
And the rat, that hunts
cockroaches in the darkness

of the dry food cupboard
and as you open
the door, leaps across
your chest and away.
And the concrete sweating

its careful salts, cuts
the blue sky and sun
dazzle, with a neon
street lamp flickering
throughout the day.

*

It means we take
the three good symbols,
wood, blood and water,
in a metal wheelbarrow
along the lawn edge,

as the yellowhammer
shortens our view
from birdfeeder to shrub;
green against red,
yellow against blue,

the colours sing and rise,
one above another.
The blue is cerulean,
receding, but always
within the frame.

*

After the night's rain,
an installation. Dockets,
counterweights and cabling,
polythene-wrapped
on pallets brought in

from wet pavements under
cloud. Assembled there,
for walling in, between
the classroom and the lounge;
between the climbing chalk,

the hamster and Jack Russell.
A grace that's clean, that warms
and salves; grace that is
voluptuous, swinging
its blue earrings.

*

To think of that dance
of hands in a small, oak-
panelled committee
room as memory,
where the door opens

to a draft that catches
transparent plastic
and runs it across
the concrete floor
of an Anderson shelter,

or a church, its smell
censed clean, a woman
kneeling in the undercroft:
the difference between
being and becoming.

2   '...them that are without'

The scene bisected
by a single point
of light which comes
in time from above,
on skin contained

in clothing or hair,
touch in a dark room.
A rook in daylight,
the Little Owl at dusk,
their wings opened

over pavement where
the fleece is dry but
the ground is wet,
or the ground is dry
but the fleece is wet.

*

This is the wool and this
the shorn sheep. Trees,
in sprays of light, sway
out from a valley side
that tips to the tidal edge.

This is the pigeon and this
the quivering squab. At ebb
the inlet is a straggle of skin
where trees close
on oyster catchers and the knot.

This is the church and this
the naked sky. All this
from the pub, a hundred feet
above tide pools,
the estuary's assertions.

*

Satraps of the sun:
dove and raven drift
towards horizons
where breezes stiffen
over waterscrew

and patient windmill.
A bucket drops to water.
From roof tops smoke
gathers and shrinks, a trace
after all that.

Again it seems
late sun gives
this perspective;
a dog untethered
on village streets.

*

If, at the crematorium,
at a point where families
leave to wait on
household gods,
or collect children,

on another hill,
a man walks a spaniel
on gouged chalk paths
past the lane-end
bungalow, down

the expected field
over rank grass
towards the winter river,
he urges the dog
to leap barbed wire.

*

Not the ghost of itself,
but a gate-leg table
opened out for breakfast
in an angle of light
that turns under the eye.

Not the candle repeating
the flame, or pheasants splashing
to roost, or fox fire
among rotted branches
an hour beyond dusk.

But as if the newly dead
were to gather and tell
a single story, or
blow cigarette smoke
towards the sharpening moon.

*

Foreshortening lets
you see both
head and feet. So,
it's not a bather
standing on the sand,

a towel trailing from
her hand. How
could it be? But
a small girl holding
an orange balloon, who

holds the hand of 'Boy
With Lollipop'.
The girl's hands move
into the picture from
outside the frame.

*

Tumbled chairs, that
awkward fervour
traced back and forth
over gesso;
always immanent

but liable to
culverting,
enforced decay,
the misperceptions
of analogy,

and the challenge
of that early light,
hardly florid
but there still between
the icon and the pixel.

*

A body abandoned,
or finished then
broken and worn away.
One hand clasps
but the fingertips

do not touch.
The other bends towards
the genitalia. A seated
figure would have been
enough but behind

there is a dark chair
and broken cloud. On
the table, a yellow
pepper recently
sliced by a sharp knife.

*

These dreams were full
of such debris[4]
and were represented
by signs from the start:
a pigeon dead

beneath the dog roses,
olive and magenta
scuffed over green;
four white gulls
and a man drowning

balanced the figures
on the cliff top;
white kid gloves
hung in local churches
to mark the death of a child.

3 '…in the seventh month…'

The function of this pond
is apprehension;
both torque and bowser.
For, beneath the surface,
under moving dust,

the sunlit water snail
spreads its foot
and beetles seethe
in their own bubbles.
What comes across

most strongly is
the clear possibility
of water plaiting
and unplaiting down
the backs of furniture.

*

Suddenly, from the adit,
a hare, pelting as if
for its life, along
the muddied runnel, past
the wash trough, across

the moor towards the beck;
no interiority
then, no chance
to metastasize
beyond the passive voice

or the taking of chances,
as under the wonderful
flight path of ducks,
a dead bream buckles
to the canal surface.

*

Water-dark clouds
over urgent water where
flood debris cushioned
the appetites of flood.
On barbed wire, leaves

hung with stream spray
and, on dun-coloured
aggregate, a new light
came to stabilize
these pale images

of something slewed
quickly from gouged grass
beside the by-pass,
a strewn pain, pith,
a streak of new earth.

*

At the lake edge,
that sparse evening
of drizzle and mosquitoes,
she had stepped
from the moored boat

and set it rocking.
There was a hand, palm
out, inside
the wet windscreen.
In the photograph,

she neither looks
nor does not
at the camera.
She went away
and there was nothing.

*

This baptism: a stone
blebbed with itself
as if newly fired,
among lithe tongues
of hostas or pelargoniums,

that keeps the early sun;
a test of silent unities
allows us to give voice.
Autumn spate on a stream
that runs by new housing,

under the road, behind
the Methodist chapel,
village bakery and red-
brick terrace; the need
for yet another breath.

*

All the way along,
the sun shone on
the undersides of leaves
and angels couldn't trick
you out of it:

the campsite smell
of warm rain, dusk
and grass; a quiet voice
as a hand rubbed canvas;
and in the river's surface

an insect buzzed
to its death and dead
might be lit from below;
a microscope slide
of limbs and old habits.

*

Taut light has gathered
around this place,
between the Hudson
and the Poughkeepsie bridge.
White clapboard house

among fir trees,
a habitation for grace;
a word and past enough.
Our fingers dabbled,
careless and quick, upon

the rowed boat's wake.
A summer rain storm
shakes the swimming pool,
and behind that voice,
the sound of yet another.

*

From the cliff top,
to the rocks below, the still
and deepening sea; where
fingertips can find
a place that is not

land or water; where
a rib cage is
and below that, skate
and seakale, and nutrients
that are vestments

too, for near all
this, are coastal towns
where seagulls
scream and dawdle over
waiting Sunday streets.

*

The duckboard dips
to the surface beneath:
each touch annealed,
cramped in faith, where
we step over

suspended matter;
foul water and mud,
the ground of our being
in so many ironies
that balance our way

to a green hide among
reed beds to witness
the Grey Lag Goose
loosen from water and lift
towards the giddy limits.

*

Beyond estate wall
and paddock, plane
tree and elm, flame
has caught the underside
of spring grey cloud.

Flood water river
fills the valley;
its flowering surface
and blunted river bed
are still. It is

the road-topped bank
and nothingness of
creatures that are the stream,
unmoralised and
unbecoming.

4 Midrash

January cloud
and sky without rain
but full of purpose.
Winter steps, mud
and dark leaves caught

against risers.
Footprints frozen
in mud and elsewhere
cycle tracks set
in gelid grass.

Memorial Gardens.
In the bandstand,
the guttering's loose
or gone, the ceiling
flakes in rosettes.

*

A lodge in civic green,
its portico
lurid with words
and down whose side
is a ginnel to urinals,

stale and telling.
Enacted stucco
clads the upper floor;
windows where
curtains rot to grime.

Behind us here,
laurel, magnolia,
rhododendron,
primrose with
its winter veins.

*

Pennine town
that pulls the moors towards
this brown slab
for Kenworthy, local
born poet, his

anxious moustache
from the citizenry.
And those who gather
by the bus stop
might or might not

know that overture,
the mind full of things;
that almost quiet
when blustery wind
has died on your ear.

5 '...one equal light...'[5]

A place not in
our racial history,
not fully brought
to self-consciousness;[6]
beyond fire and smoke,

beyond the parterre,
the walled garden, sheep
lying on the drive,
reed beds and a heron
rising to mobbing rooks;

field and hedge row,
taut horizon,
gathering distance;
this string of events
where silence is.

*

In this place are
the 1950s,
that walked a hospital
corridor in
late sunlight.

In this place are
the 1960s,
that lay under a tree,
with bougainvillea
on a south facing wall.

Think of Laocoon,
wrestling the serpents,
with and for his
sons, a tall order,
another crucifixion.

*

If that is the angel
captured up there
in gold and sunset,
above cold sands
and jostling tides,

and this is us here,
who shiver a little
in electronic music,
on the garden terrace
and wait for night

to open and rooms to be
lit, then what
drives in to be fixed
is an inward, in-
voluntary composure.

*

Train weight on wheels,
those coils of spring,
the stippled chimney
to turn diesel smoke
into the vaulted roof.

In this animation,
the image of a pigeon
looping almost
from platform three
to platform four.

A small boy kicking
a plastic cup, then
aiming a kick at that
pigeon might restrict
what you believe.

*

It's not for us to seek
or even to believe;[7]
the flies have come at last,
they join and part
beneath the arc lamp.

Sash windows have been
opened, junction boxes,
half a column of plastic
chairs beside grey
baffle screens, and note

how trees and voices change
outside the room
and the traffic. Magnolia
blooms before it
puts out leaves.

*

Run up and bowl,
Run up and bowl
in the flat quadrangle.
Twenty years later,
sit in the front seat

of a grubby pick-up
that climbs a dry track;
in the back are two
dead sheep and a woman
in full hijab.

The scaffolder's art,
'this place of the soul's
exile, precisely
its motherland'[8]
if only it knew.

*

There was the shtetl*,
and clematis to drop
white petals on June
soil; how morning
sunlight through

the carriage window
is filtered by a girl's
fair fringe. The train
slides by a hazel
that rubs brickwork,

buddleia drying
towards autumn, empty
trainsheds. In
its homeostasis,
the I contracts, expands.

*shtetl: Yiddish for a small town; commonly used
of Jewish towns and villages in Eastern Europe.

*

Moss on old slate,
lichen smears and fungus,
excluded under the soffit
a snail reads the surface
with its fondling slime.

Between render and stucco,
out of chafing winds
enough seepage to deter
the final autumn wasp
fresh from the soul of crowds.

Wasp and snail who
make their testimony
among prefabs,
hutments and leaf smoke
at the ragged civic edge.

*

What remained after
the house burned, the lawn
in silence and smoke drift,
was a compost bin,
eggshells, rot,

cabbage stalks and flies
rising and settling. That
afternoon when
the stream ran on
by chemical pools

and security cameras,
between buried sidings,
the motorway and Steel
works; the tongue left
to search behind the teeth.

*

At eight o'clock, the horses
came, animal and rider
in day-glo coats,
between pavement maples
towards the sleep of horses,

where horses kneel
or stand those hours
among the impulses
of dream. What grainy
imagery might that

be to which a human
could contribute –
tiltyard and flag,
smoke and early sun,
metaphor and habit?

6 Penitential Psalms

Here's the church and here's
the steeple; here's the priest
and here are the people and there,
on the tarmac,
are toy people who

make tiny gestures,
or walk among the planes,
or drive model cars;
and there are those
who have been taken

from their own lives,
and those whom we
know to be in
someone else's
clothing and skin.

*

A red calorgas
cylinder in a doorless
trackside shed
with buddleia and the ghost
of a passing train would

imply such and such
a human body or hill
slope under the form
of pencil or paint[9] that
had become the portion

of goods given which
is forgiveness,
and emulation,
drizzle on a slate roof
on a winter afternoon.

*

Without the dolls' house
which her father made,
which was her house,
and beyond it, is
the darkness, unreturned.

Between sunset
and sunrise when
her hair was scraped
back and her mouth
wounded, a fly became

a nest of eggs, and the dolls'
house offered more
and more light; at
once her father was
both lost and found.

*

There was a man without
possessions who saw
the balance between hand
and face; the thumb knuckle
lift to lips and brow;

fingertips to fore-
head, down and then
across the chest, and finally
the palm open on the breast
bone; who saw

the surf where you
can dance, the tide-
line where small
boys meet and call
their gang 'The Hunters'.

*

But look, it is winter,
she is old in sleep,
will do the cold thing
and stay away; the drizzle
of torment designed

to catch herself
unawares and will
not remove the splinters
from under her nails;
watches for encroachment

of all measure of dignity.
The pestle resting in chaff
and uncrushed grain, she
waits for the veil to rend,
rend to the last tatter.

*

To draw a portrait
of desire where
mystery decays
to belief is to ask
why this white

concrete box partly
bitten back to the steel
reinforcement was pitched
on its side among marram
grass by a coastal path;

or a hanging basket
is a gash of blue seen
from a car and yet on
foot is the usual mix
of lobelia and petunias.

*

This responsory:
that a man walking
at night between
two homes hears
a fox bark and thinks

of the rabbit and the fox's
sudden breath. Or,
driving on a Saturday
morning, sees hedged-
off spaces where

you might stop
and piss, and worn paths
at an angle that
run between fences
to who knows where.

*

The monastery sat. Its
blue dome bobbed
against the pines, outside
were cannons, a restless
flag. Below were rocks,

a still and deepening
sea. Across the inlet,
there they stood,
the king and queen among
the muscular houses on

the hill. But who owned
them, and the beasts they
walked between, and birds
that flickered up and off
as they walked on?

*

Under streaks of sudden
sun, along the edge
of small, northern towns,
sandwich bars
open and close, an idea

of death that is barely
entertained. Look
- along the High Street,
among catenaries,
pigeons flutter

and filaments of burnt
paper. All of it
never trying beyond
a sense of being
utterly dependent.

7 'Somewhere or other inside his head there must be an angel'
Pablo Picasso on Marc Chagall

From allotment skies,
July showers fall
to rouse young crows
among dusty branches.
The fat earth buckles.

Samuel Palmer knew
how each leaf
lies clear of the next,
in wind-held sun
where lost flies float;

the stark implications
of trees at hand, their
canopy's calm belief
in time – this week
and the week after next.

*

Has nothing changed?
Japonica rises
beside the basement window,
where a crane fly
feels cold air.

There are hands
that seem to touch
the very borders of affliction;
and a child, neat, distressed,
the wainscot, printed

paper, mouldings,
a coffered ceiling,
and clarifying skies
where gliders turn
beneath a private sun.

*

Small steps taken
on icy pavements, a hand
that slid in the dark
to the switch. With both
hands full, things

can heft from palm
to finger, along the sides
of fingers, or so
the mind might feel.
The train's upon the curve.

The ticket collector
in the next car's
lost to view but making
his way through
all that light.

*

Winter comes beside
the railway. Through
it you can see
the things that summer hid:
the nuanced English

countryside spreading
from the train, horses
bent to grazing, a hiker
squeezing by two
concrete posts

to look beyond that
gate, at understory
and coppicing, to each
indifferent east
and all the other souths.

*

A bundle of wood, a web
of aconite were left
beyond the measures
that produced the sarabande
and the gavotte; and then

the collared dove was left
among bark chippings,
in the darkness of
solemn underbrush.
Forms of life that seem

to merge with rocks at dusk
lived with the moon
behind them, and under-
water were the mollusc
and the unblinking fish.

*

Between the sawhorse
and the out-house door,
that kind of gifting
is made, to cross
the species barrier,

so 'Lightning turns
whatever it
strikes towards
itself, so a man
with his back

towards it is flung
around to face it;
all the leaves of the tree
turn over to face
the lightning stroke.'[10]

*

Three kinds of litany;
one revealed and faithful,
one traditional,
and another that works
against its mooring

through a summer of floods
and ragwort, until
a warm September
of bramble and blackberry,
when what dies

back from the river side
is a return to earlier
voices that sang, open-
throated and unbearably,
of the way things are.

*

To walk the grain of the field
in the wind rush of grass;
and follow a rising arc
to the white edge and beyond;
to trace a spoken pattern.

These are new scents
for the upland hare, above
a stream in sheep pasture
among rank bracken
and sliding stone. To ripple,

complete the shadow
and shapes behind rock,
complete and then
turn back to the start;
each strand, each wave.

Notes

1 John Vernon Taylor was a missionary statesman, ecumenist, Africanist, General Secretary of the Church Missionary Society, and later Anglican Bishop of Winchester (1975-85).

2 *o ouranos*: transliteration of the contemporary demotic Greek word for "the sky".

3 'The relation between us and God, between this world and His world, presses for recognition, but the line of intersection is not self-evident.' Karl Barth, *The Epistle to the Romans*, sixth edition (New York: Oxford University Press, 1918 [1933]).

4 'My dreams are full of such debris.' Otto Dix.

5 'Bring us at our last awakening into the house and gate of heaven, to enter into that gate and dwell in that house, where there shall be no darkness nor dazzling, but one equal light; no noise nor silence, but one equal music.' John Donne.

6 'A place not yet in our racial history, not fully brought to self-consciousness.' Simone Weil, *Waiting on God* (London: Routledge and Keegan Paul, 1951).

7 'It's not for us to seek or even to believe...' Simone Weil, *op. cit.*

8 '...this place of the soul's exile, precisely its motherland ...' Simone Weil, *op. cit.*

9 'such and such a human body or hill slope under the form of pencil or paint' David Jones: letter to Rene Hague, 19 January, 1973 from: ed. Rene Hague, *Dai Greatcoat : a self-portrait of David Jones in his letters* (London: Faber, 1980).

10 'Lightning turns whatever it strikes – whether tree, beast or man - towards itself. A man with his back towards it is instantly flung around to face it; all the thousand leaves of the tree turn over to face the lightning stroke.' Meister Eckhart, 'The Eternal Birth' in ed. H. Backhouse, *Meister Eckhart* (London: Hodder and Stoughton, 1992).

Biographical Note

Ian Pople was born in Ipswich and educated at the British Council, Athens and the universities of Aston and Manchester. He has taught English at secondary level and in higher education in Sudan, Greece, Saudi Arabia and Britain, and currently teaches at the University of Manchester.

His first collection of poetry, *The Glass Enclosure* (Arc, 1996), won a Poetry Book Society Recommendation and was also short-listed for the Forward Prize for Best First Collection in 1997.

Recent publications in
Arc Publications' series
POETRY FROM THE UK / IRELAND
edited by Jo Shapcott
include:

LIZ ALMOND
The Shut Drawer

JONATHAN ASSER
Outside The All Stars

DONALD ATKINSON
In Waterlight: Poems New, Selected & Revised

JULIA DARLING
Sudden Collapses in Public Places
Apology for Absence

CHRISSIE GITTINS
Armature

JOEL LANE
Trouble in the Heartland

HERBERT LOMAS
The Vale of Todmorden

SUBHADASSI
peeled

JACKIE WILLS
Fever Tree